Life Begins at Sixty

Liu Xuehong

 Foreign Languages Press

First Edition 2007

ISBN 978-7-119-05138-3
© Foreign Languages Press, Beijing, China, 2007
Published by Foreign Languages Press
24 Baiwanzhuang Road, Beijing 100037, China
Website: http: //www.flp.com.cn
Email Addresses: Info@flp.com.cn
Sales@flp.com.cn
Distributed by China International Book Trading Corporation
35 Chegongzhuang Xilu, Beijing 100044, China
P. O. Box 399, Beijing, China

Printed in the People's Republic of China

Contents

Life Begins at Sixty

Foreword

In April 2006, Wang Shijie retired from Shanghai Science and Technology Museum. Being accustomed to working, he suddenly felt at a loss and could not adapt to retired life. He learned from the radio that government departments in Shanghai were recruiting retired people to work as volunteers in Xinjiang. He signed up immediately. This is how he became a member of the "Silver-age Mission" and went to Xinjiang to do something useful with his remaining time.

The "Silver-age Mission" is a public welfare activity initiated by the China National Committee on Aging (CNCA). It employs retired scientists and technicians in developed areas of central and eastern China to provide intellectual support to underdeveloped areas in western China.

According to Wang Qing, director of the CNCA "Silver-age Mission" Office, China currently has more than 5 million retired scientists and technicians, including 3.5 million below the age of 70. About 70 percent of them hold middle-level and senior professional titles and are in a state of health that permits them to continue working. These retired intellectuals are a valuable asset to the country. The "Silver-age Mission" was launched nationwide in 2003 so people with expertise are able to continue to contribute to China's development. Wang Shijie is one of its volunteers.

Over the past three years, thousands of silver-age volunteers from medical, cultural, educational and agricultural backgrounds have brought their technical know-how and experience to western China. While providing technical support and working out solutions for these less developed areas, they have found new meaning in retired life.

1

Living a Meaningful Retired Life

Making a Difference: Working in Old Age

In China, the official retirement age is 60 for men and 55 for women. This is based on the Labor Insurance Regulations promulgated in 1951 and revised in 1953, when the average life expectancy in China was around 50. Today the average life expectancy has reached 73. This means that many people are still strong and healthy by the time they retire. Those in the younger echelon of the retired population would rather continue doing something that benefits society. These are the experiences of two such retirees.

Botanical Lab

No. 294 Huaizhong Road, Shijiazhuang, Hebei Province is a clean and beautiful residential compound inhabited by employees of the Shijiazhuang Research Institute of Agricultural Modernization under the Chinese Academy of Sciences and their families. Like other residential communities consisting of government offices and institutions, it is composed of apartment buildings surrounded by trees and lawns and connected by paths and streets.

In the southwestern corner of the compound there is a small courtyard behind a moon gate. Inside, a winding path cuts through a garden lush with plants of all colors and sizes. There is honeysuckle, milkvetch, Chinese thorowax and many other herbs. Tian Kuixiang, who has already retired from the research institute, walks across the courtyard, guiding a group of visitors. "It is very beautiful here in spring," he says. More than 300 species of medicinal herbs and flowers grow in the 0.1-hectare courtyard, including a cluster of rehmannia that is rooted in the cracks of a brick wall in a corner of the courtyard. It really lives up to its name "Hundred Herb Garden."

Tian Kuixiang is the keeper of the courtyard. Spending much of his day wandering around the garden has perhaps made him look much younger than his 64 years of age. He is currently president of the Hebei Province Shennong Information and Ecological Engineering Research Institute, whose headquarters are located in the courtyard.

Apart from the garden, there is also a greenhouse in the courtyard, flanked by two bungalows that serve as office rooms for the institute. Some

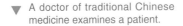

A doctor of traditional Chinese medicine examines a patient.

▲ A senior citizen helps a neighbor write some couplets for Spring Festival.

green herbs float on the surface of two small pools inside the greenhouse. The shade of green is particularly eye-catching. "This is kenaf. We are doing a vegetative propagation experiment with it." According to Tian, kenaf produces a high-quality fiber that can be used to make high-grade fabrics. Its pure-white stems are good for making formaldehyde-free plywood. If it could be grown on a large scale in sandy soil, it would be good economically as well as reversing desertification. But the problem is that in cold northern China kenaf won't bloom until October, which is too late for its seeds to ripen. The vegetative propagation experiment has yielded good results so far, but further research is needed before mass plantation.

Before Tian Kuixiang built his garden, the courtyard was an obsolete stokehold that supplied heat to the compound in winter. In 2002, Tian retired from his post as executive vice president of the institute. He cleaned up the courtyard and gradually converted it into an experiment site where retired scientists like him can carry out their own projects.

In the spring of 2004, an agri-info consultant from neighboring Langfang City came to Tian asking for technical support. At that time Tian was working with the Hebei Provincial Association of Senior Scientists and Technicians. After learning that the association had many retired scientists and technicians who hated just relaxing at home and wanted a way to use their talents, the consultancy company founded the institute, hiring Tian Kuixiang as its president.

The institute only had seven scientists in the

beginning. As the number of its projects increased, its work force expanded to the current 45 – all of them experts in agriculture, forestry, animal husbandry, fishery, water conservancy, ecology and related areas.

"We know one another very well, and it's easy for us to meet up if there is any team work needed," says Tian. "More experts help is available if we need it, as over 120 retired scientists live in the compound. More than 40 of them have received honors from the government's special bonus program which acknowledges special contributions made to the country by people of expertise."

The institute achieved a considerable amount in the few years since its establishment. Its river ecology control project has won a provincial award for achievements in advanced technology, and two more of its projects have been patented. However, this is not why Tian Kuixiang and other senior scientists continue working. They just want to live a meaningful life and do something they enjoy doing. Sometimes they get paid, sometimes not. Nevertheless, they always offer up their help as long as they have the time. "None of us talks about payment. Since we all take a daily stroll anyway, why not 'stroll' to where we're needed," says Tian with a broad smile.

A Volunteer Information Desk

"Grandpa, how do I get to the Great Wall?" asked two young women. "Walk northward for 200 meters and take Tour Bus 2," answered 70-year-old Li Guoliang.

"Excuse me, how do I get to the Exhibition Center?"

"Follow the underground tunnel to the other side of the road and take Bus 966." It was 9:30 am at the Trolley Bus 107 terminal on Beijing's Dongzhimen Street. Li Guoliang was constantly being approached by pedestrians asking the way. Sometimes he was surrounded by a small crowd.

Dongzhimen is an important thoroughfare and each day as many as 100,000 people pass through. It is a common thing for pedestrians to get lost. When they get off their bus, many head right to Li Guoliang after seeing his sign, "Directions." "Sometimes more than 100 people an hour come to ask me the way," says Li. He hardly has time to sit down as he gives directions to a constant stream of people. For complicated directions, he takes out a slip of paper and writes exactly what buses people need to take so they will not forget.

"There are a few more information desks at the long-distance bus terminal over there," said Li. "All of us are retired and in decent health so we decided

▲ A senior citizen is doing embroidery.

to offer a free guide service. It's not some great noble enterprise, just a little thing that we do."

Li Guoliang used to work in the Beijing Minerals Bureau. "I was born in Beijing and lived near Shatan and Beihai Park for decades, so I'm familiar with the city." In August 2000, Li put up his "directions" sign outside Liangmaqiao South bus stop in the eastern part of the city. In November 2001, he moved house to Dongzhimen, so he started working in the complicated street system by

Dongzhimen subway station. Except for on snowy and rainy days, Li has turned up to work every day for six years without demanding anything in return.

"My job takes a lot of know-how," says Li. Over the past six years he has accumulated a lot of experience. "The public transit routes are frequently changed, and I have to keep up with them. I sometimes buy newly issued traffic maps and I buy a few newspapers every day to keep in touch." Li Guoliang also does his own research. To get first-hand knowledge of the bus routes in Beijing, he has followed every one of them on his bike.

Working as a guide is not plain sailing. At the beginning, pedicab drivers who waited outside the subway station treated Li rudely, because they thought his service would divert their potential customers towards public transport. "Things are much better now, though, and sometimes even pedicab drivers come to me for directions," jokes Li. Of the many people he has helped over the past years, Mr. Li remembers one particularly vividly. One day a girl who had stood beside his desk for about half an hour asked him timidly how to get to Yanqing (the farthest outlying suburban county of Beijing) and begged him to lend her some money. Li didn't have any money on him so he got on his bike and rode home to get some money for the girl.

He then sent the girl off on the bus heading for Yanqing. A year later, the girl appeared with her mother, to give him back his money. She also brought him a gift. Li was surprised: "I couldn't accept their gift, but I was very happy that they had thought of me." What Li appreciates most is other people's understanding and support. "I get support from my wife. I only hope that other people will support me too."

Li has more than a dozen co-workers around Dongzhimen. One of them is 75-year-old Xie Liang, who comes to work every day despite his advanced age. Influenced by their elders, more than 50 young people have joined them as volunteer guides, ensuring that the practice will continue.

Due to the increased number of scholars and experts reaching retirement in recent years, many places have established a "Silver-age Human Talent Pool" to assist the younger of them who want to continue working. Continuing to work as much as their health allows helps old people improve their quality of life and slows down the aging process. As a result they add to the dynamism of society as a whole.

▶ The Red Twilight Cycling Club from Yibin City, Sichuan Province, visit Haikou Wanluyuan.

Enjoying Life: Fun in Old Age
Going to Africa Alone at the Age of 68

An Youzhong is a retired photographer from the China Labor and Social Security News and an expert honored by the government's special contribution bonus program. At the age of 68 he traveled alone to Uganda, without even speaking the country's language, and came back with many photos that he had taken there. He set out on March 25, 2003, carrying a pack of 30 kilograms, including a laptop and four cameras.

Africa is a mysterious and enchanting place, but it is also full of danger. Its strange languages and viruses pose great challenges to a man in his late 60s. However, its virgin grasslands, crowded slums, clear sky and lakes full of animals have a great appeal to a professional photographer like An Youzhong. And, despite his age, it was an appeal that he could not resist.

Wherever he went in Uganda, Mr. An tried to take photos of the local people's lives. That was not an easy job, as the country was socially unstable and locals either refused to have photos taken or else charged money for it. Mr. An had to take his chances and take quick and stealthy snaps, or use his connections. With the help of his friends, he met a Ugandan congressman and a mayor and

An old couple from Jingansi Sub-district, Shanghai, having a photo taken before setting off on a foreign holiday.

took their photos.

Pygmies are an ethnic group unique to Africa. There are fewer than one thousand left. They continue to live a very primitive life. Five days before he returned home, An Youzhong met a Chinese businessman who told him that one of his salesmen had a photo taken with the pygmies. Mr. An immediately went with his driver to search for them. With the help of a local guide, they found the pygmies in a few hours. Mr. An recorded their lives with his camera.

"It gives me a feeling of accomplishment to have traveled to Africa alone at the age of 68," says An Youzhong. "From the point of view of their documentary value, my Uganda photos are better than those I've taken in China, particularly those of the pygmies that I took on the Uganda-Congo border. I might be the only person in the world who has had a chance to take their photos." Mr. An stayed in Uganda for three months. After he came back, he published his book *A 68-Year-Old Photographer's Solo Journey to Africa*, which records his days in Uganda.

It was not until 2003 that An Youzhong learned to use a computer. Now he writes two blogs. Every day he updates it, reads any messages that have been posted for him and replies to the questions of his internet friends. Talking about retired life, he says that it is only now he is able to do the things he never had time for, like this trip to Africa. He feels his retired life is even more colorful and fulfilling than the one he led before.

An Youzhong has bought a car so is free to go wherever he wants. He can now make a round trip to a rural corner of Beijing within a day. He intends to make a second trip to Africa when he is 72. This time he has been invited.

An Old Couple on Wheels

When Gao Shujun obtained his driver's license he was almost 70. Now, in his early 70s, he might be the oldest driver in China. Not long ago, he drove his Engle from Nanjing to Mohe village in Heilongjiang Province, the northernmost point in China.

Mr. Gao started his motor tour of China in 2005, his wife serving as his navigator. On his latest trip to the north he covered over 10,000 kilometers there and back. A tire had to be changed but the engine held up well. Mr. Gao is the oldest motor-tourist in China. His greatest desire is to travel through every part of China and become a modern-day Xu Xiake (a famous traveler, geographer and writer of the Ming Dynasty). Of course, he'll

Senior residents of Sifu Street Community, Xi'an City, Shaanxi Province, getting ready to go on stage.

depend on his Engle to accomplish this task and to take him to Beijing for the 2008 Olympics as well.

As the standard of living in China rises, many retired people have attempted motor-tours, just like the Gaos. One such couple is Ma Youlin and his wife Li Mei, both retired middle school teachers from Xinjiang. In the 1960s the couple left their hometown, Chengdu, Sichuan to work in Xinjiang in a nationwide campaign that called young people to support the construction of China's frontier areas. After they married in 1969, they devoted their time and energy to teaching, leaving little time for travel. They longed to travel around the country, though, and see the beautiful landscape of China.

"As we got older, my wife and I became less and less satisfied with living out our days doing taiji exercises and shopping and cooking for our grandchildren. In 1997 we decided to learn how to drive, in order that we might buy a car, and travel around the country in it," says Ma Youlin. That year he was 62. Ma worked diligently in driving school, and got the highest mark in his class for the theory test. However, he was much slower than younger students when it came to the practical component. He put in the extra hours and finally passed the road test and received his driver's license.

In July 2002, the couple bought a car for RMB

59,000. In July 2003, they set out from Urumqi on their maiden tour and in a few months had seen Gansu, Ningxia, Shaanxi, Henan, Anhui, Jiangsu, Shanghai, Zhejiang, Jiangxi and Hubei, covering a total of 8,600 kilometers.

When they were on the road, they struck others as being full of life, always having a smile on their faces. One person said: "You guys are really great. You're retired but you take your car traveling just like people half your age. It's really admirable." A month later, they returned home safe and sound. "We finally fulfilled a dream we'd had for 35 years," said Ma Youlin beaming.

The Never Ending Journey: Study in Old Age

Students in Senior Citizens' Universities

Whenever one goes to Shanghai Senior Citizens' University on Nantangbang Road, one is sure to hear the sound of singing. That is just the music class rehearsing. Often mouth-watering smells float by. That will be the cookery class studying under the instruction of top chefs. The art class is holding an exhibition. Looking at the vivid animals and birds, bold plants, and magnificent colors, it is obvious the students have had formal training.

The Shanghai Senior Citizens' University was founded in 1985. Then it only had two classes of 58 students. Today it offers more than 70 courses, including history, literature, art, calligraphy, housekeeping, health, music, computing and foreign languages. In addition to 7,200 students in 228 classes at the main school, it operates 22 smaller branches across the city with a total student population of 24,000, the oldest student being 91 years of age.

Wu Shanfa used to work at Shanghai Turbine Factory. His retired life is comfortable and easy. He decided to go to the senior citizens' university to study the arts. He loves calligraphy and studies under Lin Zhongxing. Lin does not just teach calligraphy, he also teaches traditional Chinese culture, which really interests old Wu. Mr. Wu finds time to practice calligraphy every day. He finds that calligraphy not only helps pacify his mind and soul, but also strengthens his body. In addition, he reads ancient books and recites ancient poems, both of which are essential for a good calligrapher. If ever he does not understand something, he just asks his teacher. Mr. Wu feels a new man. Now his neighborhood committee often calls for his help when they need someone to pen couplets and posters, and Mr. Wu is always happy to oblige.

People often tease Qin Danhua: "If you'd worked this hard all along, you'd have two Ph.Ds by now." She has been a student at the school since it first opened and has completed over 20 courses, including literature and arts, Chinese literature, foreign literature, *Records of the Historian, Analects of Confucius*, and dance. Her thirst for knowledge has still not been slaked. People ask why she studies with such enthusiasm when she no longer needs an education to help her get on in life. Ms. Qin replies: "The school makes me feel young again, and gives me a new energy."

▼ Students at Tianjin Nankai District Senior Citizens' University listening attentively to a lecture.

▲ Senior citizens take part in an internet skills competition in Dongzhimen Sub-district, Dongcheng District, Beijing.

Yu Limei, an 86-year-old woman with silver hair and graceful manners, is the oldest student in the creative writing class. She says studying has given her a "second spring." She is also a loyal reader at the Shanghai Library. She reads books, newspapers and magazines and takes notes on them. "I've no time to feel lonely because I've got too much to study," she says.

Such enthusiastic students can also be found in senior citizens' schools all over China.

Even though the temperature was minus 6 degrees Celsius and icicles were hanging from eaves, 63-year-old Pan Li arrived early at the Tianjin Senior Citizens' University. That was the day when she and the others in the beginners' ballet class would give a public performance. Pan Li, a retired professor of physics from the Tianjin University of Science and Technology, had attended the class for three years, every Thursday afternoon.

"Ballet exercises have stretched my old limbs, improved my physical condition and even changed the rhythm of my life," says Pan as she ties the pink laces of her ballet shoes. Words cannot describe how excited she gets about ballet. Pan has injured both her knees and was forced to have an operation. Since she started her ballet training, the muscles in her legs have become stronger and she is no longer so prone to have falls. Ballet really energizes her. Whatever she does she gives it her all. "I don't expect to be a good dancer, but ballet makes my life more fulfilling. People shouldn't just give in to age" she says.

A senior ballet troupe dances gracefully to the music of the *Four Seasons*. Even if their posture is not perfect and not all the steps are exactly right, they are so absorbed in their performance and smile so beautifully that they win long applause from the audience.

At the age of 64, Zhang Shouhua may be the oldest member of a senior citizens' ballet troupe in Anhui Province, but her movements are very precise. "It was completely different when I first started learning ballet. It was torture putting on the ballet shoes," says Zhang. But in order to realize her childhood dream of being a ballerina, Zhang grit her teeth and struggled on. "Ballet doesn't just make me feel more beautiful, it even makes me younger," she says.

Piano is also popular among senior citizens. In Wuhan, there are more than 1,000 of them taking piano classes in senior citizens' universities. Most of them are retired professionals, such as doctors, teachers and engineers. Some old people play the piano to keep themselves fit and healthy, some for their emotional well-being, and some just to pass the time. Instructors teach simple techniques and relaxing pieces that old people enjoy. Experts point out that systematic piano training can help protect the heart, limbs and brain of old people who are in a reasonable state of health.

Since their inception 22 years ago, senior citizens' schools have developed on a considerable scale. There are around 26,000 nationwide with a total of 2.3 million students. Some localities have also established their own education networks which cover the provincial, municipal, county, township and village levels. These facilities provide programs which combine education and recreation for senior citizens and which have improved the quality of their lives.

Keeping up with the Times

Up until now, computer games and the internet have been the domain of young people. But in recent years there has been an increasing number of senior netizens around the country. A woman in Nanjing who identifies herself as Lengcui, or "Cool-and-Green", on the internet has become a celebrity in the virtual world.

Her name is actually Chen, she is 58 this year, and she has an eight-year-old grandson. Ms. Chen is a high school graduate. When she was young, she was notorious for following fads at her work unit. She spent her spare time dancing or playing cards, chess and table tennis. After she was married, her husband bore the brunt of most of the housework and she amused herself with even more recreational activities. She took up computer games and the internet six years ago. Ms. Chen learned to play computer games in 1995 when her daughter bought a computer. At first, she was only a curious onlooker when her daughter and her daughter's boyfriend worked and played on the computer. Later her daughter taught her to play the games. She gradually got to grips with the computer and completed most of the games. After she retired in 1998, she began to use the internet, using the very individual user-name "Lengcui." Once she had learned to use it, she found the internet more interesting than computer games, not to say conventional pastimes such as miniature croquet, mahjong, karaoke and chatting over a cup of tea. The internet

▼ Fashion show given by a group of senior citizen models from Donghuashi Nanli Community, Chongwen District, Beijing.

Stories from China

was the only pastime for her. After finishing her morning routine of exercise, shopping and taking care of her 8-year-old grandson, Ms. Chen now spends three to four hours every afternoon in an internet bar. She doesn't care about the curious and bemused stares of youngsters in the bar. "If youngsters can play *changpai* (a card game popular

among old people), why can't I go to an internet bar?" For Ms. Chen, the internet is an exciting activity that makes her feel young again.

In Shanghai, white-haired people carrying digital cameras and laptops, or browsing web pages with their palm pilots add to the charm of the city. Not long ago, more than 1,000 senior citizens in Shanghai participated in a two-month-long digital life competition designed for old people. Thirty of them won competitions in games, internet shopping and other aspects of internet life.

Shanghai is an aging city with 2.5 million citizens aged 60 or above. Having financial security, these senior citizens look forward to enriching their cultural and spiritual life, improving their quality of life and benefiting from all the advances of the digital era. To fulfill their needs, government departments in Shanghai have sponsored a "Help the Old Get Online" program by running community internet classes for senior residents. Internet-savvy senior residents help run the program. They teach their peers, step by step, how to use the internet. So far, 200,000 senior residents of Shanghai have gone through the program, 100,000 now have a basic knowledge of computing, and 500,000 frequently go online. The internet has enriched the lives of old people.

2

Living a Healthy Retired Life

Healthy Body, Healthy Mind

China has 130 million people above the age of 60, some 10 percent of the population. It is expected that by the middle of the 21st century, China's old age population will exceed 400 million, about one quarter of the national total. As health is a prerequisite for a high quality of life, in 2001 the Chinese government launched the "Senior Citizens' Fitness" campaign, encouraging old people to do physical exercise and other healthy activities. It is estimated that about 60 million old people nationwide are keeping fit.

Keeping Fit

Health and longevity become particularly important when one reaches old age. Zhang Kaiji, an accomplished architect in his 90s, has developed his own way of keeping fit.

Zhang Kaiji was in the first generation of architects to emerge in new China. He was born in July 1912 in Shanghai, though his paternal family is native to Zhejiang's Hangzhou. He graduated

▼ Famous traditional Chinese medicine practitioner, Deng Tietao, leads students in practicing the Baduanjin exercise technique.

from the architecture department of the Nanjing Central University in 1935. He worked as chief architect of Beijing Municipal Architectural Designing and Research Institute and as vice chairman of the China Architectural Society. He is now an architectural advisor to the Beijing municipal government. Mr. Zhang received the "Master Architect" title in 1990, and won China's First Liang Sicheng Architectural Award in 2000. He has designed many famous buildings including the Chinese History Museum (now renamed the National Museum of China), Diaoyutai State Guesthouse, the Tiananmen viewing stands and Beijing Planetarium.

At the age of 95, Mr. Zhang is in high spirits and very quick-witted. He has a healthy complexion and a young heart. He has a large collection of wood, bamboo, jade and bronze carvings and sculptures. His wood carvings include human and animal figurines, miniature houses and bridges, and window and door panels. They are extremely impressive. All these intricately made carvings are decorative components of ancient Chinese architecture, either used to decorate the eaves, rafters, doors and windows or to be displayed inside. Mr. Zhang says he collects these items for two reasons. Firstly, they are good examples of architectural decoration and are pleasing to the eye. They can, therefore, help him better understand the style and practice of ancient architecture. Secondly, they help his emotional well-being and bring him happiness. "Joyful and carefree, one can live forever," smiles Mr. Zhang.

When it comes to keeping healthy, Mr. Zhang believes that one's physical condition depends very much on how well one takes care of one's body and soul. To keep a peaceful mind, a modest attitude, an optimistic outlook and to stay away from worldly worries will help ensure one's spiritual health; while physical well-being relies on activity. He reasons that exercise of the muscles and bones lead to smooth circulation and a strong body. That explains why "Life depends on activity." Mr. Zhang thinks that, even if his age means he cannot do strenuous activity, he should not give up exercise altogether. Walking has been part of his daily routine for many years. It helps strengthen the muscles and bones and improves circulation sending nutrients to every part of the body. Mr. Zhang never demands nor sets exercise targets for himself. He does what he feels capable of. He describes it as "Letting nature be the guide."

Zhang Kaiji also loves traveling. He always advises his friends to spend more time outdoors

▲ Residents of Nanleili Community, Dongnan Sub-district, Yuyao City, Zhejiang Province, celebrate Zheng Benkun's 100th birthday.

when conditions allow it, so as to see more of the world and enjoy the beauty of nature. He says such experiences will broaden their horizons, enrich their life, and help with their mental and physical health.

Happiness Leads to Longevity

It was 9 o'clock on October 28, 2004, a beautiful morning in rural Rugao – a county famous for longevity in China. Zhang Tianshi, a 105-year-old

▲ Elderly women play on a swing.

woman, walked out of her room to greet a group of visitors who had just stepped into her courtyard.

"I'm very busy these days. The county government just called, inviting me to attend an event tomorrow," says Zhang. From the look of her, it is clear that Zhang still likes to have fun. Her grandson Zhang Desheng adds: "The day before yesterday, she insisted on seeing off a visiting aca-

demic from the Chinese Academy of Social Sciences."

"I get up at 6:30, sweep the floor, take a walk, and then come back to do the laundry and cook lunch. I take a nap around 4 or 5 o'clock in the afternoon and have supper at eight... I've never taken medicine nor had injection. I can walk three kilometers to my daughter's home without the help of a walking stick." The centenarian's mind is clear and her words unconfused.

"My eldest son runs a grain store. I sometimes help him by answering the phone. I can remember how much grain a caller wants and what price he'll pay for it just by listening to him once." Zhang Tianshi speaks of her memory with great pride. Her grandson says she is a woman of simple pleasures:

▲ Senior citizens from Xizhuang Village, Baoshan City, Yunnan Province, take part in an embroidery competition.

Stories from
China

"She likes watching TV. She can't understand what's going on, but she is happy enough comparing the beautiful faces. She is happiest on her monthly theater day when she goes to see a folk opera."

When asked how much longer she expects to live, she answers: "So long as my mind is sound, I'll stay out the ground." After she lost her father, Zhang Tianshi was sent to the Zhang family as a child bride at the age of 15. She has given birth to eight children. "Those days were really hard," recalls Zhang, unemotionally. "If I can avoid illness, I'll live for a while yet," she adds.

Qiu Ruxing, a 100-year-old man, lives in Apartment 201, Building 102 in the Hongjiyuan area of the urban district of Rugao. Since he has a bad hearing, her daughter Qiu Dongmei speaks for him most of the time. He lies in his cane chair on the balcony, soaking up the sun.

"He won't just stay at home doing nothing. He loves chatting with friends and neighbors, playing chess and watching TV. He goes out for a walk around 8:30 every morning. First he throws his walking stick downstairs, and then holds onto the railing and walks down the steps," his daughter explains. Qiu Dongmei describes her father as good-tempered except for when he plays chess. "He's determined to win. A few days ago, he had a game with an 88-year-old friend. They had a fight about certain move and eventually just stormed off."

▼ Competitors in a calisthenics competition in Nantong City, Jiangsu Province, perform Mulan "Two-Circle" dancing.

▲ Senior citizens from Tongzhou District, Beijing, climb a hill.

Qiu Ruxing does not seem as enthusiastic as Zhang Tianshi about parties. Qiu Dongmei says: "His birthday is on Double Ninth Festival. Except for his centenary this year, he has never celebrated his birthday, saying that it is a day when his mother suffered. However, he was very happy at his centenary banquet and even penned a few characters for the occasion." Although he lives with his daughter and granddaughter, Qiu Ruxing does not need special attention. His life is simple – two bowls of rice for lunch, some porridge or noodles for breakfast and supper, and a few vegetable dishes and bean curd. Qiu Dongmei says that her father never asks about family affairs, but he is interested in what goes on in the wider world. "He's recently been asking me about the latest developments in Taiwan."

In a dim, old house at the end of an alleyway, 100-year-old Lu Xiuying is getting ready for lunch. When she looks up, the two bright eyes that shine brightly from her wrinkled face are very affecting. Her 69-year-old daughter Jia Furu recalls: "When my mother was young, she was really beautiful and her complexion was very pure."

Lu Xiuying has her own philosophy on life. "She fights with us to do the housework, particularly washing dishes and vegetables," says her daughter. "She always washes her own clothes. Five or six years ago, she was still smoking a water pipe, and had a glass of rice wine every day. She believes that as she was born in the year of snake she can't do without water." Jia Furu says that her mother is very introverted. She does not like watching TV and seldom talks with others. "She likes playing cards. She'll play by herself from morning till night." According to Jia Furu, her whole life, Lu Xiuying has only contracted one illness – typhoid – and she seems relatively unconcerned about death. "When my father died 20 years ago, my mother shed no tears. She just carried his pillow to her bed."

In the eyes of her neighbors, Lu Xiuying is a kind-hearted old lady. Jia Furu talks of her mother's centenary banquet: "27 members of my family belonging to five different generations came round for the occasion. The neighbors came over as well to share her "longevity" noodles – we had to move the banquet to a restaurant."

Two decades ago, there were only six centenarians in Rugao. Today there are 209 of them, 167 of them are women and 80 percent of them live in rural areas. Their physical condition is generally quite good: 35 percent of them are capable of taking care of themselves and 30 percent are only partially dependant on others. Most of them used to be manual workers. Of the 42 men, nine were carpenters, three were bricklayers, and four pulled wooden carts. The rest were farmers. Most of the women worked in the fields and did housework. They hardly received any education. Apart from three who went to private schools, they are all illiterate. Many of them were still working in the fields in their 90s. Physical labor has helped slow down the aging process.

Peace of mind is the key to old age. These centenarians are not fussy about what they eat and wear, they are not avaricious – they are easy going. Their secret is simply this: he who lives happily lives longest.

Exercise and Cherish Life

Life Depends on Activity

On the 2006 Double Ninth Festival, the five-month-long Jiangsu Province Senior Citizens' First Annual Sports Festival came to a close in Suzhou. Since June 10, old people from across the province have spent a happy five months taking part in various kinds of activities specially designed for them, including fun sports, competitions, and exhibitions of sports-themed stamps and photos.

Unlike a regular sports meet this festival took place over a long period of time, allowing the old people to spend five months of fun. The event requires a lot of activity but only a little expenditure from local authorities. The provincial government has decided to make it a regular annual event, to be hosted by a different prefectural-level city each year. The host city will be a meeting point for those involved in senior sports across the province. The festival opens on June 10 and closes on the Double Ninth Festival every year. It lets a huge number of senior citizens see the benefit that can be had from sport and exercise.

In mid-1980s Jiangsu became the first province in China to be classed as "aging." Today there are 11 million senior citizens in Jiangsu, accounting for one-seventh of the provincial population. Their families know very well how important their health is in terms of the family's psychological, physical and financial state. It also has a key role to play in building a harmonious society. Activities and exercises are without doubt the best way to ensure that old people live a healthy and happy life.

According to *Sketches of the Lives of Senior Citizens in Jiangsu* issued by the provincial statistics department, less than half of the 11 million senior citizens do regular exercise, and 45 percent of them never do any exercise. Of the senior citizens surveyed, 8.75 percent describe themselves as "healthy," and 36.25 percent as "comparatively healthy." When combined, this figure matches that of those who do regular exercise.

Now the question is how do we entice senior citizens into the sports ground? Yan Zhengming, chairman of the Jiangsu Province Senior Citizens' Sports Association and vice director of the provincial sports bureau, says that old people have ample time for outdoor activities once they retire from their job. More and more people realize that, no

▼ Senior villagers from Wulong Village, Zhanggong District, Ganzhou City, Jiangxi Province exercising.

matter what job they had, manual work is no substitute for physical exercise. Jiangsu leads the country in terms of economic and social development so there is no excuse for not providing opportunities for old people to do sport. The key lies in how effectively this is organized.

All 13 large cities in Jiangsu have established senior citizens' sports associations, so have 66 of its 68 counties and county-level cities and 80 percent of its rural townships. All the urban communities and most of villages have also set up their own senior citizens' sports organizations.

With effective organization, the construction of sports facilities provides a good base for senior citizens who want to do exercise. The provincial sports bureau requires that every county should have at least one gymnasium, one stadium (with a synthetic running track), one indoor swimming pool and one sports center, in addition to a number of alternative facilities enabling senior citizens to do exercises. Today a network of sports facilities has been established in all areas across the province.

Improving Quality of Life

Everyone gets sick at one point or another, never mind the more vulnerable elderly population. Disease is nothing to be afraid of; it is how we deal with it that counts. This is particularly the case when one contracts an incurable disease such as cancer, where the psychological and spiritual condition of the patient may play a critical role. To fight this dreadful disease, many places have organized "Fighting Cancer" groups. Their members encourage each other and try to stay optimistic in order to regain confidence. Together they fight the illness and in so doing prolong their lives.

When the Fighting Cancer Group in Jinan City was founded in July 2003, there were over 50 members. Today there are nearly 300 members, the oldest of them in their 80s. When you see them, you can't believe that they are cancer patients. "Does any of us look like a cancer patient," asks Li Zhanglin, who is in his 50s. "We live as happily as any healthy person." Mr. Li has both cancer and diabetes. Due to their special experience, he and his friends at the group have a deeper understanding of life than most healthy people and have learned to cherish life.

Wang Zhigang, 67, joined the group in the winter of 2003. She was a scientist with a research institute in Jinan before her retirement. She interprets the aim of the group as "To prolong the life of cancer patients and improve their quality of life." Now as deputy director of the group, she often organizes get-togethers where members share their experiences fighting cancer. She also teaches them a song, *Heroes in the Battle Against Cancer*. She hopes that all cancer patients will learn to sing the song, which she believes will give them the strength and confidence to fight the disease. The song goes: "If cancer and death are one and the same/ How is it that we're all still in the game?/ And don't say that it's all hardship and pain/ Our days are so happy, you won't hear us complain./ Yes, we'll fight on every step of the way/ And for life and for love we will keep death at bay."

Han Dabai, 62, was a policeman before his retirement. He helped found the group and has suffered from cancer a long time. As its director he handles the daily affairs of the group. He also runs a farm in Qingdao. "Director Han's farm has a large crop of sweet potatoes which are good for cancer patients. Every year we go to his farm and get sweet potatoes to share among cancer patients," says one of Han's friends in the group.

The group often organizes health lectures to teach cancer patients scientific restorative techniques. It operates nine restorative exercise centers for cancer patients at Thousand-Buddha Mountain, the Botanical Gardens, Daming Lake and other public places. After the daily exercise,

A senior citizens' exercise club from Lhasa City, Tibet, performing Taiji Shan.

they can chat and share techniques they have found helpful. The group also negotiated a discount for its members at all of Jinan's parks. They can now buy an annual pass for RMB 60. "Now we can organize regular tours to these parks, which help with the recuperation of cancer patients," says Wang Zhigang. She continues: "The cancer patients get chemo- and radiotherapy in hospital. In the group they get social therapy. When we add a proper diet and traditional Chinese medicine to the mix, our members have an 80-percent survival rate."

Li Zhanglin has great faith in the group's social therapy. Although he has intestinal cancer and needs daily insulin injections, he is recognized as the comedian of the group. He can always make those around him laugh and his sense of humor is very infectious. Compliments are always an important part of his social therapy, as they can give cancer patients confidence, help relieve their mental pressure and rekindle their desire for life.

Incomplete statistics shows that cancer patients belonging to such organizations have a five-year survival rate of 55 percent, five- to nine-year survival rate of 38 percent, 10- to 19-year survival rate of 13 percent, and 20-year and above survival rate of 4 percent, which is markedly higher than cancer patients outside these organizations.

3

Living a Happy
Retired Life

As children grow up, and as the world changes, there are many elderly families in Chinese cities who either have no children, or whose children live away from home. A new term has been coined for such families – "empty nests." According to an investigation, 59 percent of these "empty-nests" involve people aged between 60 and 74.

As their physical condition deteriorates, old people may find it more difficult to take care of their food, homes and medical issues if there is

▲ Senior resident Li Yufeng happily eats the dumplings given to her by her community committee in Jinfeng District, Yinchuan City.

nobody to look after them. The three major problems they face are loneliness, a lack of help around the house and a shortage of money.

"Empty nest" families are a result of the aging population and of certain social changes. As more big families choose to split up into nuclear families, the number of "empty nests" will increase. If social services cannot keep up, the lives of old people will be adversely affected. To tackle this problem, many Chinese communities have experimented with welfare programs.

Community Help for the Old

"Empty Nests" Need No Longer Be Lonely

On the morning of October 1, 2006 over 40 residents living in an old people's home named Xiyang Honghuo – meaning roughly "the setting sun is also bright" – in the West Lake Community of Hangzhou gathered with their families to celebrate National Day and the Mid-Autumn Festival. They staged performances they had rehearsed and really got into the spirit of things.

The home is new, and sits in the shade of surrounding trees. Its residents, all above the age of 65, seem as happy as children. They sit all around the grounds, leaving the center free to be used as a stage. The program includes a singing competition and games like picking up small glass balls using chopsticks and blowing up balloons.

Grandma Li is a warm-hearted lady in her late 70s. She moved into the home in June 2006, and often tells other residents how she came to make friends. With support from the management of the home, she founded the Xiyang Honghuo Service Team and issued, on its behalf, an open letter to all the senior residents of the city. The letter says that the team members are committed to sharing their

▼ A senior citizen who lives alone (left) chats and exercises with a nurse in Chang'an Community, Wuhan City.

happiness with senior residents around the city and to making friends with "empty nest" old people. They can call them up or come round for a chat and listen to what is on their minds.

The West Lake Community has over 500 elderly residents who do not have children around. Most of them used to lead a lonely life. To meet their need for social contact, the community has opened a hotline. When old people need help, they can simply dial the number. The community has also organized the younger echelons of the elderly community into a network of volunteers to pair up with the older residents and see to their emotional needs. The neighborhood committee members regularly visit the "empty nest" residents and to ask how they are getting on. This work helps to build bridges between community residents and wider society.

Zhou Aihui is one of many senior residents who have received community help. Both her son and daughter live in the United States. She had always been a lively character, but her husband's death in 2003 changed that. She became very lonely and seldom went outdoors. The community paired her with a senior volunteer named Peng Caiyun. Peng and Zhou soon became good friends and shared everything with one another. Zhou gradually recovered her lively spirit and became the lead dancer in the community drum team. Her son wanted to send her a computer from the United States to relieve her boredom, but she turned it down. "I'm having a lot of fun. There's always some activity going on and community cadres are always available when I need them," she told him.

Family-style Old People's Home

The Laoshan Dongli Community in Beijing's Shijingshan District has introduced a family-style old people's home for its "empty nest" residents, offering all sorts of services.

The family-style old people's home is an old people's home that comes to you – that is to say volunteers come to help you in your own home. But who is qualified to apply for this program? And who will cover the costs?

The community requests that applicants be over 60, have no living spouse or any children living at home and have difficulty taking care of themselves. If they require part-time care workers, professional medical attention or medicine they must pay for such services at the usual rates. However, the community demands no payment for day to day management and services.

The family-style old people's home provides a

wide range of services: they create and update medical records on all participants; provide an annual health checkup; organize quarterly lectures on physical and psychological health, healthy eating and exercise therapy; offer consultations; provide help with household chores; and offer free haircuts. They also organize quarterly trips, entertainment events, and reading groups.

Both Song Yuqing and his wife are 76 this year. They are among the first group who applied for

▼ Senior residents in their senior residents' community activity center. Some play Chinese checkers and some play with building blocks.

the service. Song says that, though they are still able to take care of themselves, there are times when they do not feel well and need help. Their two sons and their daughter are busy with their work and do not come back on workdays, even if they call their parents often. When the children saw the community service business card and learned that their parents had joined the program, they were very happy.

After learning of the service, many local residents and students from nearby schools have been inspired to get involved with the program and work as volunteers to help with cleaning and window washing. They are really popular with the old people using the service.

Ninety-one-year-old Grandma Yu lives by herself. Her neighbors lend her a hand by picking up shopping for her, but cooking is something that Grandma Yu finds troublesome. Since she joined the program, her 70-year-old neighbor Ning Wenfeng has started helping her with it. Last week, Grandma Yu said she missed dumplings. Ning immediately went to buy ground pork and vegetables. When they learned what she was doing, the neighborhood committee members also came to help Ning make dumplings. Grandma Yu ate the delicious dumplings smiling from ear to ear.

▲ Senior residents from Xinxing Beili Community, Tianjin, learning Chinese painting at their senior residents' community care center.

Helping Senior Citizens Living Alone

Now single old people living in the Fenghuang Sancun Community of Nanjing City don't have to worry about where to find their dinner, since the community has opened a dinner service for them. The community committee members came up with the idea when they saw that many single elderly residents had difficulties cooking a proper meal for themselves. Since August 2006 the members have taken turns to shop, cook and promptly deliver

▲ Senior residents from the Nanshan Group Old People's Condo, Longkou City, Shandong Province, playing pool.

▲ A 100-year-old resident at Wuxi City Old People's
Home, Jiangsu Province, wishes a 110-year-old
resident a happy new year.

meals to these residents' homes. The service now
has eight regular diners.

　　To express his gratitude for their service, 91-

year-old Zhai Jinlun sent a silk banner to the committee. The banner was made by Zhai Xuedong, Zhai's son who is in his 60s. Since father and son live far away from one another, the son can only bring food to his father once every three days. The community committee has done the son a big favor by making sure his father gets a hot meal every day.

Most old people living alone are frail and frequently ill. They are prone to accidents like the sudden onset of an illness or a bad fall. As old people often live their lives behind closed doors, it is hard for others in the community to find out how they are doing. To address this issue some communities in Nanjing have invested in "emergency call buttons." These are installed in the homes of the older residents, so whenever they are in trouble someone will soon be there to help them. Now ten single senior residents in Fenghuang Xincun and Mochou Xinyu communities have such a button by their bed. Once, Grandpa Chen in the Mochou Xinyu Community had a fall and badly hurt his face. He pushed the button for help, and very soon the community cadres arrived at his door and took him to hospital. Grandpa Chen was very grateful. He said that if not for the button, he might have bled to death without anyone's knowing.

Senior citizens talking in the Jiu'an Old People's Condo, Nanxun City, Zhejiang Province.

Apart from the 30,000 people above the age of 80 who live in the 500 old people's homes in the city, Nanjing has 2.6 million people above the age of 60, 166,000 of them living alone. To help with their lives, local communities pair them up with volunteers who visit them regularly and offer needed help.

According to the head of the Longchang Community Committee in Nanjing, the community now has 21 single senior residents and all of them have been allocated volunteers to help them. Many senior residents said words could not express the consideration they are shown by these volunteers. So long as the volunteers are around, there is nothing to worry about.

Old People's Condos as a Solution

In China working couples usually have four elderly people to look after – parents and parents-in-law. Some might even have eight, if their grandparents and grandparents-in-law are still alive. However, with their jobs, it is very hard for them to provide adequate attention and care. Nowadays, many elderly people in such cases have opted to live in old people's condos to relieve loneliness.

Seventy-five-year-old Grandma Chen is a retired teacher from the Foshan No. 18 Primary

School, Guangdong Province. Not long ago, she moved into an old people's condo. Previously, she lived with her eldest son and daughter-in-law. Though they were both good to her, they left for work early in the morning and came back late at night. Grandma Chen was home alone during the day. She felt lonely and restless and often spent the day walking round the apartment – from her bedroom to the sitting room, from her sitting room to the kitchen.

One day she heard about a nice old people's condo. The next day she paid it a visit to check it out then announced that she had decided to move there. This completely took her children by surprise. Her children said there was no way – other people would accuse them of not even being able to look after their own parents. Because of their objections, Grandma Chen was not insistent. Some time later, however, she brought the topic up again, saying that no one could deprive her of the freedom to make her own decisions. She got her own way. Her children and grandchildren often visit her at the condo and are pleased to see that she is really much happier there than staying at home.

Chen Cuilian is an 86-year-old Hong Kong resident, but Foshan is her hometown. She moved into the condo two years ago. Both her sons work in Hong Kong and have no time to take care of her. Since she has a daughter who works in Foshan's Nanhai District, and the old people's condos are much cheaper in Foshan than in Hong Kong, she decided she would live out her days in Foshan.

Chen Cuilian stays in a single room. It has an air-conditioner, color TV, refrigerator and hot water. She hires a maid to take care of her. Apart from watching TV and reading the paper, her main hobby is calligraphy which she practices every day. She also enjoys chatting with the other old people in the condo. She is satisfied with her life in there and says that she has no regrets living there.

Old people's condos have become popular in recent years. Shen Bin, a professor of sociology from Zhejiang University, says that solitude directly affects old people's health. In cities, people live their lives behind closed doors and there is little communication among neighbors. This situation exacerbates their solitude, which, in turn, affects their physical and mental health. In a condo old people are able to communicate with one another. There are a lot of people their own age to talk to and they can start on a new and happy life.

This choice of life also indicates a change in old people's social attitudes. They no longer judge their children in terms of whether they are filial or not. Now they've found happiness in living well and not being a burden on their children.

Medical Services for the Old

Home-based Medical Service

As one gets older, it gets harder to avoid falling ill, but going to see a doctor can be inconvenient for old people. When it is a serious illness then it is simply a case of being admitted to hospital. But if it is a chronic illness requiring frequent check-ups and repeat prescriptions, then old people have a lot of difficulties. Now hospitals in many cities have started offering home-based medical service for such patients.

The home-based medical service offers checkups, treatment and care to patients that meet its requirements. Doctors visit them regularly at home and bring them medicine. This system is unique to China. It makes up for the shortage of sickbeds in hospitals on the one hand, and saves the hospitalization cost for patients on the other. So it is considered an effective alternative to hospitalization.

The Chinese Ministry of Health issued regulations on the management of the home-based medical service as early as 1984. These stipulate that people covered by the medical care system will be entitled to claim as much back on their medical insurance when they receive home-based medical care as when they visit hospitals. In the 21st century, this new form of medical service has been promoted across China to the benefit of millions of old people.

One fine morning in Guangzhou, Huang

▼ Doctors from Jinxiuyuan health center in Yinchuan City, Ningxia Hui Autonomous Region give "empty nest" senior citizens a physical checkup.

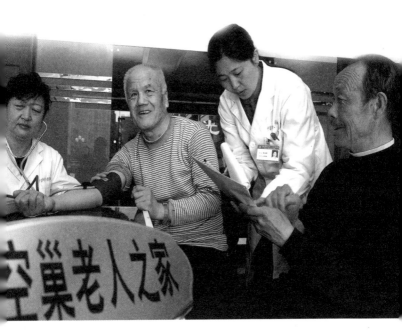

Liangyu, a 25-year-old medic from Dongshan District No. 2 People's Hospital, set out on his weekly visits to his home-based patients. He had three patients to visit before lunchtime.

His first patient is 77-year-old Grandpa Yang, who had a thyroid cancer operation a few years ago. In addition he suffers from high blood pressure, diabetes and heart disease. In the previous two years, Grandpa Yang has been hospitalized several times because of two strokes. His condition is stable now and he does not need to be hospitalized, but still needs frequent check-ups. Last year, Grandpa Yang applied for the home-based medical service, and Doctor Huang visits him once a week.

Doctor Huang's second patient is 88-year-old retired teacher Jin, who lives by herself. She is infirm due to cerebral atrophy, and the functions of her other organs are also deteriorating. She has received house-calls for two years.

The third patient is Grandma Zhong, who has high blood pressure and cataract. Doctor Huang visits her once a week and, since she has poor eyesight and has no one there to look after her, brings her medicine.

The service provided by home doctors in Guangzhou does not only cover regular visits and prescriptions, but also injections, drips, acupuncture, massage, the redressing of wounds and taking of samples for lab tests. Depending on their condition, community medical stations also do ECG examinations, basic physical therapy, therapeutic clyster, spray treatment, ultrasonic diagnosis B, fundus examination, and stomach and intestinal examinations for home-based patients.

Generally, a home visit costs RMB 15 to 20 – large hospitals might charge double that. This expenditure is not covered by medical insurance, and patients have to pay by themselves. Hospitals also charge more to home-based patients for treatment and medicine than patients who go to the hospital. The method of payment for the service varies depending on the types of patient, that is to say, whether they receive free medical care and whether they have medical insurance or not.

Deathbed Care

According to the WHO definition, deathbed care refers to all sorts of active care given to terminally ill patients. Therefore deathbed care is both a medical and social undertaking that shows people's respect for life coming to an end.

This service appeared in China's interior areas quite late. In 1987, the Songtang Hospice was founded in Beijing. It was China's first private hospice. In 1998, Li Ka-shing donated money to Shantou University Department of Medical Science No. 1 Hospital for the establishment of a hospice, and promotion work has since been stepped up across the country. So far, 20 large hospitals across China have founded hospices as a result of donations from Li Ka-shing. Every year he invests as much as RMB 20 million. Apart from the one attached to Shantou University in Guangdong Province, the 20 hospitals include the Beijing Tiantan Hospital, Beijing Cancer Hospital, Shanghai No.2 University of Medical Science's Xinhua Hospital, Tianjin No. 1 Central Hospital, and Shenyang University of Medical Science of China No.2 Hospital. While alleviating the physical pains of advanced cancer patients, these hospices also provide emotional and spiritual consolation.

The hospices admit patients who have less than six months to live. It is not their job to cure the illness, but to control pain and manage symptoms to improve the patients' quality of life. In this way patients can face death calmly and live their last days with dignity.

Most of the patients in the hospices are above 80 years old. They live with a personal nurse who helps them with washing, shaving, bathing, eating,

▲ The staff and residents of the Minxing No. 2
Old People's Home, Yangpu District, Shanghai.

and going to the toilet, as well as giving them daily
massages, talking with them, singing them songs
and telling them stories – it all helps to lessen their
fear of death. The background, character and condition of the patients vary, so do their needs. The
hospices treat them on an individual basis.

Eighty-two-year-old Grandpa Xu has high
blood pressure and diabetes. Previously, he had
been hospitalized several times and his family was

told his condition was critical. Finally he got so distressed that he pulled out his oxygen tube. His family had no option but to send him to a hospice. With the help of a professional nurse, he has calmed down and become cooperative. He says that in the hospice he feels his life is meaningful, as everyone there is working for his benefit and he feels their affection for him. He says he would have no regrets even if he were to die today.

4

Facing the Aging Issue

Tackling Aging Before the Economy Has Fully Developed

According to international standards, a country or a region where 7 percent of the population is above the age of 65 and 10 percent above the age of 60 is considered an aging region. France was the first country to be classed as aging. Since then around 70 of the 190 countries and regions of the world have been classed as aging.

Statistics from the Ministry of Civil Affairs show that China is an aging country: 134 million

Chinese citizens are above the age of 60, comprising for more than 10 percent of the population, and 94 million above 65, more than 7 percent of the population. By 2025, the number of Chinese people above the age of 60 is expected to reach 300 million.

The aging population poses great economic, social, political and cultural challenges to China and exacerbates the pressure on its care, medical and social services for the aged. In 2004, China's basic pension expenditure was RMB 350.2 billion, an increase of 65.5 percent from 2000, and the central treasury's subsidy expenditure on basic pension increased to RMB 52.2 billion. Expenditure on retired people has increased sharply for several years in a row. The government, businesses and social institutions already feel the increasing burden of taking care of the old.

It is estimated that old people spend three to five times more money on medicine than young people. In the current transitional period – as government functions are being re-examined and adjusted and the function of the family as the basic unit in taking care of old people is being weakened – the development of the service industry for the aged has fallen behind the growth of the aging population. The situation is particularly serious with the "empty-nested," those of very advanced age

▲ Residents of the "Red Twilight" Old People's Home in Hefei City, Anhui Province, wipe icing on a friend's face to his great delight.

and with invalids. Taking welfare institutions for old people as an example, China has 38,000 of them, averaging nine beds for every thousand old people. This is compared with the average 50-70 beds for every thousand old people in developed countries.

The aging problem is even more serious in rural areas. The number of elderly people in the countryside is greater than that in the cities. The majority of Chinese villagers are not covered by a pension system, and the new cooperative medical care system is still in its experimental stage. The countryside still lacks the welfare system to deal with the aging population. As the aging process speeds up, the pressure on daily care and medical services for the old will be more severe in villages than in cities, particularly in the western provinces and poverty-stricken areas. The solution to this problem depends on economic development and the joint efforts of government, social and family sectors.

Experts believe in the 21st century the aging trend of China's population will be unavoidable. Between 2001 and 2100, there will be three stages:

Stage One: China will see a rapid aging period between 2001 and 2020, when its senior population will increase by an average of 5.96 million a year, or 3.28 percent, as compared with the 0.66

percent growth rate for its total population during the period. By 2020, China's senior population will reach 248 million, accounting for 17.17 percent of the total population; and those aged 80 or above will amount to 30.67 million, or 12.37 percent of the senior population.

Stage Two: China will experience an accelerated aging period between 2021 and 2050, as people born during the second baby boom of New China in the 1960s and early 1970s enter old age. During the stage, China's senior population will increase on average by 6.2 million a year. As the national population goes from a zero growth rate to a negative growth rate, the aging of the population will increase. By 2023, China's senior citizens will number 270 million, the same as the 0-14 age group. By 2050, their population will increase to 400 million, 30 percent of the national population. The population aged 80 or above will be 94.48 million, or 21.78 percent of the senior population.

Stage Three: There will be a stable but significant aging period between 2051 and 2100. By 2051, China's senior population will reach its apex at 437 million, approximately double the number of children and young teenagers. During this stage, the senior population will stabilize at 300-400 million, around 31 percent of the national population. The proportion of the people aged 80 and above will remain between 25 and 30 percent of the senior population, making China a highly aging country.

The aging issue is more serious in China than in developed countries because it has hit China before China's economy is sufficiently advanced. The Chinese government is actively dealing with the problem at all levels and utilizing all its social resources to explore effective living and medical solutions to ensure a happy and worry-free life for old people.

▼ 82-year-old Liu Yuqiu (first, left) eating moon cakes with the other residents of Hepingli Old People's Home, Beijing.

The Government Foots the Bill

Forty years ago, her miserable marriage forced Zhang Jianying to flee her hometown in Henan's Wenxian County. She stayed with her brother and sister-in-law in Zhengzhou's Jinshui District. After her brother and sister-in-law died, Zhang Jianying, then in her late 70s, lost her means of support. Since her registered status as a permanent rural resident could not be changed, she was not entitled to receive subsistence allowance for the urban poor. For several years, she had to make a living by picking out recyclables from garbage.

In 2004, the Jinshui District Civil Affairs Bureau dispatched a domestic helper to Zhang Jianying, and her shabby and solitary conditions have completely changed since. In the past, it was a challenge for Zhang to get herself three meals a day. When she went to buy vegetables, she would always plant the roots in flower pots on her balcony. When she was unable to buy vegetables, she would pick a few leaves from the pots to put in her noodles. Though the pots on her balcony are still green with celery and coriander, she no longer has to rely on them as her "vegetable garden." "Now with Xiao Wang (her domestic helper), I don't need to worry about buying vegetables," says Zhang. "The neighborhood committee also provides me with rice, flour and cooking oil, so now I have meals to eat, as well as someone to talk to." All the domestic service bills for Zhang Jianying are footed by the government.

According to the Jinshui District Civil Affairs Bureau, all single senior citizens like Zhang Jianying are given a complaints phone number. If three complaints are lodged against a helper he/she will be dismissed by the bureau. To guarantee good service for the elderly, the bureau has also organized a supervision team to check on the quality of domestic service and find out about people's service needs. Jinshui District has 98 single senior citizens. All of them are provided with free domestic services for between one hour and three hours a day depending on their age. The service includes washing, cleaning, chatting, massaging and any other chores around the house that are requested. Each helper gets paid RMB 6 per hour. The personnel training and salary is paid for by the government.

Apart from the free service program for single residents above the age of 60, Jinshui District also plans to institute a subsidized domestic service program for "empty nest" couples above the age of 60, providing an hourly subsidy of RMB 3.

Jinshui District learned of the program from

Nanjing. In Nanjing the municipal government pays for a professional community service system. They operate a new type of welfare system for the aged – family-based welfare for old people. Nanjing's Gulou District has 100 single senior residents. The municipal government allocates RMB 100 per resident to pay for a professional community service system. They send trained helpers to do housework for senior residents for no less than 20 hours a month.

Now many local governments provide free domestic services for their senior residents who require it.

In 2006 the Wuhan municipal government in Hubei Province implemented a scheme whereby the government provides 365 hours of domestic and nursing services a year for its oldest single citizens. Anyone who lives alone and who is above the age of 80, who is disabled and above the age of 70, or, if their children receive an urban subsistence allowance, whose monthly income is lower than RMB 460 are entitled to the service. The hour-a-day free service includes washing, cooking, cleaning, shopping, accompanying the elderly to see the doctor, reading books and newspapers to them, and chatting.

The Beijing municipal government has published a paper on service for the old, *Proposals for Home-based Services for Old People*. The paper stipulates that the government will cover the costs of domestic and nursing services for four groups of old people: urban and rural old people who have no means of livelihood other than subsistence allowances and who are incapacitated or partially incapacitated; old people in families whose per

▼ Senior citizens who enjoy the "five guarantees" (food, clothing, medical care, housing and burial expenses) visit a new senior citizens' service center in Yangshe Town, Zhangjiagang City, Jiangsu Province.

capita income is higher than Beijing's poverty line but lower than its minimum wage of the current year and who are incapacitated or partially incapacitated; people above the age of 60 who hold an award as a model worker conferred by the municipal level government or higher, or who are returned overseas Chinese and who are incapacitated or partially incapacitated; people between the ages of 80 and 89 living alone and who are incapacitated or partially incapacitated, old people between the ages of 90 and 99 living alone and all people aged 100 or above.

To prevent accidents during working hours when single old people are alone at home, the Xi'an municipal government in Shaanxi Province has installed an emergency call system. When they fall, get ill, or have other accidents, or when there is a fire, elderly citizens can push a button on a watch-like remote control worn on their wrist that will activate the call button installed on their telephone. A city service center is able to identify the name, age and address of the caller and then sends emergency help.

According to incomplete statistics, more than 20 provinces and regional authorities have implemented government-funded and subsidized home-based services for old people living alone. In addition, many localities have launched volunteer programs for the aged. Thirteen million volunteers have provided 630 million hours of service for 2.8 million old people.

Provision for the Aged Through Property Arrangements

Over the past two years Shanghai's Hongqiao District has been experimenting with a "service bank" old-age welfare scheme. Younger senior citizens in good health volunteer to care for the oldest members of the community. The hours they put in are tallied up and, when they get older, they can reclaim the same amount of free service.

In Beijing, some "empty nest" old people rent out their housing and use part of the rent to pay to live in old people's homes and similar institutions. Grandma Jin, who is in her 70s, is a retired office worker. She has an apartment in Zuojiazhuang, Chaoyang District. All her children moved out of her apartment when they started their own families. Grandma Jin found it inconvenient to live by herself and could not find a satisfactory maid. After thinking it over with her children, she decided to rent out her apartment and use the money to move into a nice old people's condo in the suburbs. She looked at various places and eventually found a suitable one run by the local government: the rooms are clean and hers has a color TV; there are people to take care of the residents; the air is fresh; there are plenty of people to talk to; and the condo organizes lots of activities, like sports days. Grandma Jin's eldest son helps her collect her rent. After paying the condo rent, she still has some money left over. The family is still as close as ever – her children and grandchildren come to see her on weekends, just as when she lived alone in her apartment. Moreover, her children don't need to constantly worry about her. The condo has 12 residents like Grandma Jin who rent out their apartments. In the past, old people had to rely on their children for financial support if they wanted to stay in old people's homes. It is a mental relief for old people in Grandma Jin's situation that they can foot the bill themselves and still have some money left over.

The private Wenquan Liuyuan Old People's Home in Tangshan Town, Nanjing, borrowed a "retroactive payment" old-age care system that originated in developed countries. If they sign over the deed to their house to Wenquan Liuyuan, old people are allowed to stay in the home free of charge benefiting from the full service package. When they die, Wenquan Liuyuan then comes into possession

of their house. This old people's home was the first to adopt such a system in China. Different versions of housing-based old age care system have appeared in Beijing and Shanghai. Wu Yiming, director of the Nanjing Normal University Social Work Research Center, explains that as a complete and well-financed old age care system is yet to be

▼ Senior Citizens who have already moved into the Red Twilight and Chaohu Old People's Condos in Hefei City, Anhui Province.

established, the housing-based old age care program is good temporary solution to the problems
posed by the rapid aging of the population

Many other localities around China are also
exploring practical methods of old age care. One
scheme has appeared in certain parts of rural Henan,
where like-minded single old people are organized
into small groups. The government then builds
houses for them to live in and they can share their
twilight years with one another. This eases financial pressure on the government as they do not need
to provide individual housing and saves the old
from loneliness. By taking care of each other senior citizens are also able to rediscover the warmth
of a family atmosphere.

The "Warm Project" in the 012 Courtyard of
Shifang Village, Gaocun Township, Yingyang,
Henan Province has caught many people's
attention. The courtyard is composed of five rooms,
with three men living in them. "Big Brother" is
70-year-old Zhang Huqun, "Second Brother" is 72-
year-old Zhang Shunqing, and "Third Brother" is
63-year-old Zhang Maogang. Zhang Huqun is still
in good shape, can cook and is happy to look after
the other two. Zhang Shunqing has some trouble
with his legs but is still able to look after himself.
He is in much better condition than the very frail

Zhang Maogang so gets placed second.

This newly formed family is one of Yingyang's experimental projects helping single senior residents to help themselves. According to Zhang Jinhai, head of the Yingyang Municipal Civil Affairs Bureau, the government provides an annual living allowance of RMB 1,000 for each member of these households, in addition to an annual subsidy of RMB 200 given by their village and production team. Each of these households is allocated farmland. The head of the production team subcontracts this land to willing farmers. The senior residents will receive 150 kilograms of wheat each year in return. The village is responsible for covering bills for minor illness, while the township government will cover bigger bills. Zhang says that such an arrangement reduces management costs as well as enabling single old villagers to help one another, find companionship and live a better life.

The aforementioned Zhangs are Shifang villagers. As Zhang Huqun says, they have been friends since childhood. However, they all used to live a solitary and monotonous life. In July 2005, floods wrecked both Zhang Shunqing and Zhang Maogang's houses, and damaged Zhang Huqun's house. After the floods receded, the village and township governments discussed living solutions for the two homeless Zhangs. Both refused to live in an old people's home. Since building a house for each of them would cost too much, the villagers' committee then came up with the idea of asking the three to live together. It would save money and the three men would have companions. First they consulted Zhang Huqun. He happily accepted the idea and proposed that his damaged house could be renovated into a new home for the three. The other two Zhangs were also happy with the idea.

With RMB 12,000 allocated by the township government and RMB 3,000 from the village, villagers built a five-room house on the site of Zhang Huqun's old house. A two-room house for one man would cost RMB 6,000. So, if they had lived separately, the total cost would have been close to RMB 20,000. Looking after each other in this way has three advantages: it saves money, the houses are reusable, and it helps old people avoid loneliness. Collective housing is popular with the old and eases the financial burden of the government.

"The village cadres care about us. They often drop in to see if we are ok, and have coal sent to us in plenty of time for winter. All the villagers are ready to help whenever we ask," says Zhang Huqun. Since the three old men moved in together, their house has been visited by cadres and other villagers every day.

In the past, when Zhang Shunqing lived alone, he had to cook and wash for himself, struggling all the time with his painful legs. When he was ill, he could not even get himself hot water to drink. Now Zhang Huqun often helps him by massaging his legs and cooking for him. Talking about their current life, Zhang Huqun beamed: "Eating at the same table and having someone to chat and joke with helps us enjoy our food and heightens our spirits. Living together makes it easy for us to look after one another. For example, when anyone feels unwell, there is always someone to call for a doctor, and give him food or hot water and so he'll get better much quicker. If someone tried to separate us now, none of us would agree to it."

Silver-hair Real Estate

"Third housing" is a new term that has appeared in the real estate sector in the last two years. According to Ma Fengli, a researcher from the Chinese Aging Science Research Center, the Fifth Global Conference on Aging held in 2000 in Buenos Aires divided a lifetime into four stages. People between 60 and 85 years old belonged to the third stage. This is behind the concept of "third housing,"

▲ Two disadvantaged senior citizens in Shanghai
are all smiles with their charity health cards.

which targets this group trying to satisfy their needs
for old-age care, medical service, education, work
and recreation.

Taiyangcheng – Sun City – in Xiaotangshan in
the northern suburbs of Beijing is a "third housing" project. Its interior is designed with the needs
of old people in mind. For example, the door uses
an electronic lock. A resident only needs to swipe
their card and it will open automatically. The apartment is installed with an electronic call system.
Even the lift is designed to be spacious enough for
a hospital bed. The community has its own hospi-

tal and a domestic service team that specializes in old-age care. According to Ma Fengli, such real estate projects are rare in China.

People living in Sun City live a pleasant and happy life. If they don't feel like cooking, they can call domestic service and get meals delivered. If they need milk, they can have it brought to their doorstep. If they're looking for entertainment, there is a reading room and a board-games room. If they want to go on a trip, there are four shuttle buses running into town a day and electric cars within the community that pick up any resident who hails. Every week there is a cultural activity and all sorts of sports and games. The community established the Beijing Sun City Hospital in cooperation with the Xuanwu Hospital for the Elderly Clinic and Research Center. The hospital gives a free physical checkup to senior residents every year and keeps a medical record on each of them. The community also runs an emergency service station in cooperation with the 999 Emergency Center offering emergency services for its residents.

The Oriental Sun City in Shunyi District was erected not long after Xiaotangshan Sun City. Its environment is full of natural interest. It sits on a 160,000-sq-m river network of ecological significance, has a 750,000-sq-m golf course and

467 hectares of woodland. The density of negative oxygen ions in the air (like vitamins in the air) is 2,000 per cubic meter, which is 40,000 times higher than in the city center. All this makes it a perfect place for old people to live.

The first residents have moved into the new Sun City, most of them accomplished senior scientists and men of letters. "Setting the pace in retired life" is the catch phrase used by the complex. There are all sorts of morning exercise clubs, including street dance for middle-aged and old people, taiji boxing, taiji fan, taiji swordplay, ballroom dancing, swimming, indoor ball games and golf. After breakfast, they can go to classes at the residents' university. There is also a farming area in the community. Residents can rent a plot for RMB 200 a year and plant whatever they like. Many senior residents enjoy this taste of farm life.

"Third housing" real estate falls short of market demand, indicating the great potential for this niche of the market. Projects like Sun City have attracted the attention of real estate developers and prospective investors. Many private entrepreneurs in Zhejiang Province have invested in building condos for old people. They believe even if they are dealing with people in their twilight years, it is only the dawn of this bourgeoning industry.

Wenzhou City, Zhejiang, was the first region to begin privatizing its welfare system, which was previously the financial responsibility of the state. With larger financial investment, a number of large, high-class and hotel-style condos for old people have appeared in the city. Over the past few years, the number of welfare institutions for old people in Wenzhou has increased from 68 to 378. Apart from 14 government-run institutions and numerous old people's homes and day care centers run by rural townships and villages, there are 125 private old people's condos within the urban area.

Unlike government investment, which tries to save money by utilizing and converting what is already available into old people's homes, private investment operates on an impressive scale. Most of its projects are large, high-class, hotel-style condos. Early this year the Zhejiang Silver-hair Real Estate Development Co., Ltd., in association with the Zhejiang Ma Yinchu Welfare Foundation, constructed a residential area for retired people. The RMB 260 million project covers 20 hectares, 60 percent of which are made up of garden areas. The buildings offer a total floor space of 100,000 square meters. It is composed of condos, townhouses, a recreational area, a medical center, and an international communications center. It is a garden-style residential area built especially for old people providing living, health, recreation and holiday making functions.

Protecting the Lives of Senior Citizens and Safeguarding Their Rights and Interests

Li Bengong, deputy executive director of the China National Committee on Aging, gave a report on China's old-age welfare development at the State Council Information Office news conference on December 12, 2006. The white paper *The Development of China's Undertakings for the Aged* was issued concurrently.

Li Bengong says that the year 2006 marks the 10th anniversary of the promulgation and implementation of the Law on the Protection of Rights and Interests of Senior Citizens of the People's Republic of China and is the first year of the implementation of the 11th Five-year Plan for the Development of Undertakings for the Elderly. As a developing country, China's basic national situation is characterized by a large elderly population which is rapidly growing and by unbalanced economic development. Looking at the reality of the situation the government has set development objectives for senior citizens. They must be taken care of, have easy access to medical, educational and recreational facilities, and have the opportunity to use their experience to benefit society. To realize these objectives, the Chinese government has taken a series of measures to guarantee the legal rights and interests of senior citizens and has made clear progress in coordinating the development of senior citizens' enterprises with the country's economic and social development. The main achievements are as follows:

1) A basic legal and policy framework for senior citizens has been established. Over the past two decades, the National People's Congress and its standing committee, State Council, ministries and state commissions have promulgated over 200 laws, regulations and policies concerning senior citizens. The central government has promulgated the Law on the Protection of the Rights and Interests of Senior Citizens of the People's Republic of China. Thirty provinces, autonomous regions and municipalities directly under the central government have drawn out their measures to be taken to implement this law and to regulate for the protection of senior citizens' rights and interests. As a result, a basic legal and policy framework concerning the social security, welfare, service, health,

culture, education and sports, as well as the protection of rights and interests of senior citizens and related industries has taken shape.

2) Plans have been made and implemented to promote the development of senior citizens' enterprises in coordination with the economic and social development of China. China started to implement age-related development plans in 1994. In the 11th Five-year Plan for the Development of Undertakings for the Elderly promulgated in 2006, the Chinese government announced the objectives, tasks and measures to be taken for each stage of development. Departments under the State Council and various levels of local government have subsequently worked out their plans of action. Meanwhile, the state has established a statistical index system and a supervision and evaluation system. This will monitor and gauge the development of age-related enterprises in China and facilitate scientific planning and effective implementation.

3) The organizational network for age-related enterprises has taken shape. In October 1999, the State Council set up the China National Committee on Aging to plan, coordinate and guide work around the country. The committee is chaired by a vice premier, and comprises 26 ministerial-level state departments as its member units and a vice

minister from each of the 26 departments as its members. The committee has set up an office to take care of its daily operation. The committee has set up subordinate branches on provincial, municipal, prefectural, county and township levels. The villagers' and neighborhood committees, as the grassroots administrative units for rural and urban areas, also have responsibilities concerning senior citizens.

4) Social forces have been directed towards enterprises for the benefit of senior citizens. The

▼ Residents' representatives at the founding ceremony of the Hepingli Senior Citizens Association, Beijing.

government utilizes market structures to encourage and support enterprises and institutions to develop diverse products and services for senior citizens. It directs social forces and propels national and local organizations and societies for senior citizens to set up foundations, organize large-scale recreational activities, conduct age-related research and develop education for the benefit of senior citizens. It also encourages grassroots and volunteer organizations to provide diverse services to facilitate the daily lives of senior citizens and enrich their cultural and spiritual lives.

5) The lives of senior citizens are guaranteed and their rights and interests protected.

The urban and rural old-age security system has started to take shape. In recent years, the Chinese government has gradually instituted a basic pension program that covers urban employees of all sectors. By the end of 2005, 175 million people were insured and 43.67 million retired people were drawing pensions. Meanwhile, the government has tried to expand the financial resources of the basic pension fund and increase the finances allocated to the growing aging population. To protect the rights of senior citizens in rural areas to receive care and help, a petition for an "Agreement on Family Care and the Support of Senior Citizens" has been conducted in villages across the country. Meanwhile, the state is actively developing other welfare systems for the aged. So far, 1,900 counties around the country have launched rural pension programs. Senior villagers in need have been given preference. As proposed in the family planning policy, the central and local treasuries have also arranged a bonus fund for rural couples who have one child or two daughters, so that when such couples get to 60, they will receive a living allowance. By the end of 2005, 1.35 million people were benefiting from the fund.

A relief system for impoverished senior citizens has been established. China has established an urban minimum living standard guarantee, which provides subsistence allowance to urban families whose per capita income is lower than the local poverty line. In 2005, 22.33 million impoverished urbanites, including senior citizens, received subsistence allowances. Almost all those qualified for the allowance are covered. In rural areas, the government has implemented a temporary relief system that provides aid in kind to families in need at certain times of the year. In areas where conditions allow, the government has actively explored a rural minimum living standard guarantee system. So far, 8.65 million villagers are

▲ A couple joining in with the "Red Twilight Honeymoon" activities. They are renewing their vows on their golden wedding anniversary in a traditional Chinese ceremony.

covered by the temporary relief system, and 9.85 million by the rural minimum living standard guarantee.

Efforts have been made to strengthen medical care systems for senior citizens in both urban and rural areas. The state has established a basic medical insurance system for urban employees that is jointly funded by the government, employers and employees themselves. Those insured under this program will be exempted from the personal contribution when they reach retirement age, while the proportion of their medical expenditure covered by their insurance and the monthly medical grant they receive will be increased. By the end of 2005, 37.61 million retired people were covered by the system. The state also issues medical subsidies to public servants, subsidizes large medical bills and offers supplementary medical insurance for enterprises, in an effort to reduce the burden of medical costs on senior citizens. Meanwhile, a new cooperative medical care system has been introduced on a trial basis in rural areas. By the end of June 2006, the medical care system covered 495 million of the rural population. In pilot areas, 73 percent of the local senior population had made use of the system. The accelerated introduction of urban and rural medical care systems has helped relieve medical problems for senior citizens. Today, 31 provinces (autonomous regions and municipalities directly under the central government) have established rural medical aid systems.

Efforts have been made to speed up the establishment of community health systems in cities. Government bodies at various administrative levels have transformed grassroots medical institutions around the country into community health centers. Among other things, these health centers are responsible for the health care and treatment of senior citizens. By the end of 2005, there were more than 15,000 urban community health centers: 95 percent of cities above the prefectural level, 86 percent of urban districts and some county-level cities provided community health services. These grassroots medical institutions provide home-based medical and nursing services, as well as day-care and hospice services for senior citizens. Now some of the basic health problems affecting senior citizens can be solved within their community. The government is also actively promoting healthy-living awareness with attention to the particular needs of senior citizens. It has also taken measures to improve the prevention, early diagnosis and treatment of diabetes, cardiovascular, cerebrovascular and other common chronic diseases affecting senior citizens. Beginning in 1991, the Chinese government included research on the prevention and treatment of diseases affecting senior citizens in its national science and technology development plan. Currently, there are over 50 gerontological research institutions.

Service networks targeted at senior citizens have developed rapidly. Beginning in 2001 and lasting for three years, the Chinese government carried out the "Star Light Project", which aimed to develop community welfare and service facilities for senior citizens. Thirty-two thousand "Star

Light Centers" have been established. These community-based centers have provided domestic, emergency, day-care, convalescent, cultural and entertainment services for 30 million senior citizens. In 2005, there were 1.32 welfare centers for senior citizens in every urban community nationwide; and there were 39,546 old people's homes and similar institutions around the country, 29,681 operated by rural townships.

There has been progression on the field of cultural enterprises catering for senior citizens. China has 670,000 senior citizens's activity centers in urban and rural areas. Public cultural facilities are open to senior citizens free of charge or at discounted rate. By the end of 2005, China had 24 newspapers and 23 magazines designed for senior citizens. In total, their respective circulation was 2.8 million and 3.058 million copies. There are also many films, TV programs, plays and books aimed at senior citizens. Government authorities at various administrative levels are actively organizing cultural activities for senior citizens.

The initiative shown by senior citizens getting involved in social development is highly valued. The state has tried to create opportunities for senior citizens to put their expertise to further use. In cities, 38.7 percent of senior citizens have participated, at one time or another, in social welfare enterprises, and 5.2 percent have remained in employment. In rural areas, 36.4 percent of senior citizens are still engaged in agricultural production. Under the guidance and support of the government, 13 national associations have been organized for senior citizens, such as the Chinese Senior Professors Association, the Senior Scientists and Technicians Association and the Senior Lawyers Association. Now branches of these associations can be found across the country. By the end of 2005 there were 317,000 senior citizens's urban community associations and rural village associations in rural areas. They play an important role in getting senior citizens involved in community development, social welfare activities and the protection of their own rights and interests.

There have been advances in the legal protection of the rights and interests of senior citizens. During the 10th Five-year Plan (2001-2005), taken as an annual average, legal services provided free legal aid to senior citizens in more than 40,000 cases, represented senior citizens in over 400,000 litigation and non-litigation cases, and mediated more than 400,000 disputes involving senior citizens. Judicial departments also assist senior citizens going through legal processes. In 2005, more than 30,000 senior citizens received free legal aid.

Li Bengong points out that there are still problems and shortcomings concerning enterprises for senior citizens and that there is still a lot of work to be done in solving these problems and advancing age-related enterprises. Currently China's aged population is growing at an average annual speed of more than 3 percent. Confronted with this serious aging issue, the Chinese government will take more active and effective measures to ensure age-related enterprises can progress in synch with economic and social development and that senior citizens can share the fruits of China's progress.

图书在版编目（CIP）数据

生活到老：英文 / 刘学红著；汪光强译.
— 北京：外文出版社，2007
（国情故事丛书）
ISBN 978-7-119-05138-3

I.生... II.① 刘...② 汪... III.老年人 - 生活 - 概况 - 中国 - 英文
IV. D669.6

中国版本图书馆 CIP 数据核字（2007）第 157542 号

作　　者　刘学红
责任编辑　余冰清
翻　　译　汪光强
英文审定　John Mcmillan　贺　军
封面及内文设计　天下智慧文化传播公司
执行设计　姚　波
制　　作　北京维诺传媒文化有限公司
印刷监制　冯　浩

生活到老

*

© 外文出版社
外文出版社出版
（中国北京百万庄大街 24 号）
邮政编码　100037
北京外文印刷厂印刷
中国国际图书贸易总公司发行
（中国北京车公庄西路 35 号）
北京邮政信箱第 399 号　邮政编码　100044
2007 年(32 开)第 1 版
2007 年第 1 版　第 1 次印刷
（英）
ISBN 978-7-119-05138-3
10-E-3813P